THE ART OF MODERN DESIGN

I0803331

THE ART OF MODERN DESIGN

THE INTERIORS OF JAMES MAGNI & JASON KALMAN

WRITTEN WITH JACQUELINE TERREBONNE

INTRODUCTION

HISTORY REPEATED

Commissions are rarely simple. There is an extraordinary amount of effort that goes into translating someone else's wants, needs, and dreams through the lens of your creativity. Often you're asked to do things you've done before. When faced with especially challenging projects, I sometimes think of Michelangelo and the Sistine Chapel. He spent four years, all alone and seventy feet in the air, creating the ceiling frescoes, his masterpiece. I must admit that our work is never quite that daunting, but I do find it just as fulfilling.

With each project, Magni Kalman Design similarly sets out to create a masterpiece for our clients. Our commissions range with their specific needs, preferred architectural style, and location; however, the Magni Kalman Design tenets remain consistent: We enjoy the excitement produced by the sense of gradual reveal that you experience upon entering our spaces—something we call "the foreplay." With a carefully curated handful of forms, we create crisp, tailored silhouettes that honor the architecture. Finally, the end results exude a refined simplicity, because we put as much thought into what we add to a space as to what we edit out.

Each of us has our own style, our so-called brushstroke. Magni Kalman Design's is to meaningfully juxtapose concrete, steel, and stone with bronze, wood, velvet, and silk. In doing so, we create a lush, refined experience. The final element of that experience is the art that defines each project. Educating our clients about contemporary art and collecting alongside them is a consistent practice in our work. It is said that art changes your life. We witness this transformation in our clients as art brings a new dimension to the rooms they inhabit every day. It elevates their experience of living in their home to unimaginable heights.

Just as the creation of the Sistine Chapel ceiling frescoes was a multiyear process, designing and building custom private residences does not happen overnight. Our clients recognize this and embrace the long journey. During that period, we develop a common language and come to understand each other on an extraordinarily deep level, forming a close bond and yielding sacred spaces brimming with soul and personality. We are immensely grateful to work with such wonderful people, who give us the chance to answer our life's calling.

As any creative person reading this book knows, myriad opportunities to make art surround us every day. This book is filled with homes that are built upon our skills and efforts, our heart and soul. They are our art.

—JAMES MAGNI

PACIFIC PALISADES

THE ART OF CRAFT

While modernism is most often associated with the machine-made, the sleek, and the shiny, one special project in Pacific Palisades allowed us to offer a different expression. By crafting almost every detail of this residence over seven years of construction from ground-up to completion, we realized our clients' dream for a home that speaks to both their holistic approach to life and deep passion for travel. Every element—from the material selection to the furniture curation—was approached in an intensely thoughtful and deeply collaborative way with the homeowners. As a result, the twenty-thousand-square-foot house not only complements its spectacular site—on two-and-a-half acres of land with views of both the Pacific Ocean and the Santa Monica Mountains—but also lives up to it.

Both inside and out, the homeowners' appreciation of handmade shapes and earthy materials is reflected in everything from the grandest gesture to the smallest detail. Limestone and louvers set apart the facade of the home, and as one moves inside, those features continue in a more refined expression utilizing a higher degree of artisanship. This seamless integration came from a strong partnership with the architecture firm ShubinDonaldson. The interior dividing screens enable flow through the large open-plan space while creating an air of mystery. The unique winged shape of each slat furthers the organic feel of this traditional Japanese architectural device. This curved form also punctuates the home's most dramatic element: the staircase. Seeming to hover over a reflecting pool lined with smooth pebbles, the stair is composed of sculpted mahogany treads—their beauty multiplied by the water below and echoed in the adjacent Sean Scully painting, among the first art acquisitions for the home. Harmonious and ethereal, this stair was one of the first interior elements developed, and it truly sets the tone for our design.

The living room nearby reinforces that level of refinement with a mix of furniture layered with a symphony of influences and styles. Midcentury Finn Juhl and Gio Ponti pieces coexist with Magni Home Collection and bespoke pieces crafted in extremely rich materials such as cast bronze, rosewood, and cast glass. Without question, the most dramatic piece we custom-created for the space is the Mondrian chandelier, a radiant composition of bronze and crystal shades measuring fourteen feet by eight feet. At that scale, it acts as a second ceiling—bringing the volume down to something cozier than its twenty-six-foot height.

Moving upstairs into the more private spaces, a sense of intimacy and protection, two qualities important to our clients, prevails. A central courtyard gives their children a safe, contained place to play—another reference to Japanese design. It's on this level that we also crafted a modestly sized primary suite at the clients' request. They didn't want an overwhelming space—instead we opted for a luxuriously curated one that aligns with who they are. Hand-dyed silk from India forms a ravishing nook acting as a headboard and is flanked by Murano glass pendants. It speaks to the precision of our style that a global approach need not equate to maximalism. The entertaining floor below also picks up on their experiences abroad but with a decidedly more boisterous spirit, complete with a painted ceiling that took four months to complete, bright Moroccan tiles, and nineteenth-century inlaid doors from India. While these cues are present throughout the house, they are most pronounced here. The clients' travels have influenced their tastes, which allowed us to dig into a more cultured approach, a distinction of the worldly view of our design practice. Weaving these far-flung inspirations together resulted in this unique version of what we call Global Modernism.

PAGE 6: The earthy tones of the limestone- and teak-clad residence in the Pacific Palisades perfectly align with its staggering views of the Pacific Ocean and the Santa Monica Mountains. **PAGES 8–9:** The twenty-thousand-square-foot home is broken up over multiple levels and nestled within a two-and-a-half-acre property. **ABOVE:** Louvers and slats are recurring motifs in the design. **RIGHT:** Hand-carved treads, their cadence echoed in a nearby painting by Sean Scully, add a sculptural quality to the stair.

ABOVE AND OPPOSITE: The spacious living room is divided into distinct conversation areas furnished with a combination of Magni Home Collection furniture, collectible midcentury modern finds, and pieces that reflect the homeowners' global travels.

Caravaggio
Leonardo da Vinci
WRIGHT
WRIGHT
WRIGHT

OPPOSITE AND ABOVE: The breakfast area provides a sophisticated gathering space with a captivating indoor-outdoor quality. A live edge wood segment of the kitchen island highlights the sense of materiality present throughout the house.

PREVIOUS: A series of louvers act as seductive dividers between the living and dining areas. **OPPOSITE AND ABOVE:** The dining room is colorful and congenial with artworks by Albert Oehlen and Rebecca Horn, a cove lighting detail that echoes the shape of the dining table and emits a flattering glow, and inviting banquettes.

PREVIOUS: On the mezzanine, the exterior louvers become an important feature of the interior. **ABOVE:** A hay bale hermetically encased in glass commemorates the homeowner's father (in addition to serving as a cocktail table). It was the last bale he made before retiring. **OPPOSITE:** The earthy palette of the home plays off the expansive blue vistas of the Pacific Ocean.

OPPOSITE: The web of curves that makes up a Magni Home Collection table is a foil to the linear quality of the exterior architecture. The painting is by Ryan Sluggett. **ABOVE:** The primary bedroom was intimately scaled, at the homeowners' request. Details such as Indian-influenced pendants flanking the bed and a headboard featuring Thai hand silk-screened fabric speak to the couple's love for travel. **OVERLEAF:** The scheme of the lower level's entertaining spaces reflects a Moroccan influence. Pierced metalwork lanterns, textured fabrics, and deep red tones generate a sophisticated and theatrical atmosphere.

ABOVE, OPPOSITE, AND OVERLEAF: Water is an important element throughout the house, including in the reflecting pool under the stair, the swimming pool with its multitude of depths, and the illuminated fountain that spills down the exterior stairs.

FOLSOM

NATURAL BEAUTY

Nature can be immense and majestic and then a moment later intimate and detailed. For this grand contemporary home, we sought to strike that same balance by embracing the power of its voluminous spaces while layering in warmth through thoughtful materials. The clients, he a ceramicist and she a photographer, understood that connection as they possess a deep passion for hiking, biking, and skiing and had chosen the lakefront site in Folsom, outside Sacramento, for its proximity to nature.

They enlisted Paul McClean of McClean Design for the architecture of the ten-thousand-square-foot home. It was our first collaboration with him, and our working relationship has grown ever since and led to several other projects together. His siting of the structure and use of water features maximized the home's relationship to the landscape. We amplified that linkage by carefully placing outdoor sculptures to encourage further investigation. At the front of the house, a glistening Jeppe Hein sculpture beckons as it seems to float in a pool of water. Partially wrapped by a glass hallway, the sculpture can be viewed from multiple angles from inside. On the lake side of the house, a Jose Dávila work acts as an exclamation point at the end of the infinity-edge pool, drawing the eye out to the lake beyond. Both pieces are excellent examples of what can be achieved when clients trust us to help them build an interesting art collection with a strong viewpoint.

Inside, the influence of the Northern California terrain prevails with floor-to-ceiling windows along with the warm mix of stone and wood. Cream split-face limestone lends itself to the modern aesthetic while introducing texture appropriate for the locale, along with tongue-and-groove cedar ceilings, silver travertine countertops, and bleached-oak floors. All these elements come together in the great room, which is at the core of the home and comprises the living room, kitchen, lounge area, and breakfast room. All the areas had to feel connected and flow while being distinct enough to signal the division of space. Without that visual separation, the space would feel unwieldy. To achieve that, each section has its own anchor. The living room is centered on the patinated steel fireplace we designed. The lounge is focused on the colorful Tomás Saraceno, which hovers above a gathering of Jiun Ho chairs and our Magni Home Collection Vita cocktail table. And the kitchen is defined by warm wood cabinetry tucked into the stone.

The client wanted something sleek yet not too contemporary. To achieve this, the architecture and interiors had to be in perfect harmony—introducing warmth and earthiness with building details as well as fabrics and furnishings. We believe in blurring the lines between architecture and interiors with our designs, and this home is the perfect example of how all of the pieces can fit together so naturally. Every aspect—inside and out—feels balanced, collected, and perfectly edited.

PAGE 32: The expansive residence is separated into smaller sections to create a human-scale experience. **PREVIOUS:** With extensive frontage on Folsom Lake, outside of Sacramento, this ten-thousand-square-foot house is sleek and contemporary while exuding warmth and livability. **ABOVE AND OPPOSITE:** A sculpture by Jeppe Hein hovers above a pool at the entrance. Its reflective surface relates to the surrounding glass and plays off the rough stone.

MO
TH
ER
MOTHER
MARCEL VAN OOSTEN

THE BIRDS OF AMERICA
MAGNI MODERNISM
AVID HOCKNEY MY WINDOW
TASCHEN

PAGES 38–39: In the great room, blue accents such as the Warren Platner chairs and throw pillows on the contemporary sofa pick up on the lake's palette. **PREVIOUS:** A patinated-steel fireplace surround fabricated by Metal Art Concepts brings warmth and drama to the room. Shelving to its right displays the homeowner's own ceramic creations. **OPPOSITE:** A work by Tomás Saraceno hovers above a furniture grouping including a Magni Home Collection cocktail table. **ABOVE:** In the kitchen and breakfast area, materials used for cabinetry and counters mirror the rest of the space—making its functionality almost disappear.

PAGE 44–45: The dining area is defined by the Quasar chandelier, which seems to hover weightlessly above the table. **ABOVE AND OPPOSITE:** The main corridor acts as a gallery for the couple's significant art collection, which includes work by Callum Innes (positioned at the end of the hall), Annie Lapin, and Jean-Baptiste Bernadet.

ABOVE: The primary bath evokes a spa with its view onto a verdant courtyard as well as the elevated pairing of travertine walls with limestone flooring. **OPPOSITE, TOP:** In the primary bedroom, an upholstered headboard faces a fireplace surmounted by a painting by LeeAnn Brook. **OPPOSITE, BOTTOM:** Custom display niches showcase treasured pieces. **OVERLEAF:** The outdoor kitchen features all the elements of a fully loaded indoor kitchen—making it a favorite gathering place.

RIGHT: A sculpture by José Davila punctuates the lake view. **OVERLEAF:** The ingenious shape of the swimming pool carves out several distinct seating areas and features a curved infinity edge that extends the vistas of the lake.

DALLAS

CLEAR VISION

When a designer is faced with bold architecture, there are three possible approaches: First, the interiors can disappear completely, submitting to the structure. Second, the plan can veer toward furniture and furnishings that compete and even distract from the building's intent. Our preference is always for the third avenue, which is to respond to the architecture. This approach creates a harmonious dialogue between the two, in which the interiors support the narrative of the building through all elements, including the overall layout and every material selection, as well as the shape of each piece of furniture.

For a home in Dallas's Preston Hollow neighborhood, we looked to its modernist form and glass-and-concrete structure to inform every choice. Designed by Austin-based architect Scott Specht, the home packs a punch. It has impressive Texas-sized proportions defined by broad horizontal planes that echo the flatness of the landscape and is accented by crisp lines that magnify those traits. The house unfolds in an equally specific manner. Approaching the front door, you pass through an entry courtyard surrounded by large glass panels. Almost immediately, the homeowner's office comes into view. Reacting to this unique sequencing, we created a one-of-a-kind, freeform desk, which resides there as an expertly framed sinuous sculpture.

From there a strict cadence of rooms progresses—each one as exposed as the next. We continued with the selection of sculptural pieces, each carefully curated to hold their own within the rigorous architecture. Additionally, we looked to furniture that references the International Style (from which the house draws inspiration), including Milo Baughman swivel chairs and an Ib Kofod-Larsen Elizabeth chair. A black, solid-marble Magni Home Collection table titled Uovo, which we placed in front of the fireplace, seems more like a work of art than a functional object, as does the curved, stainless-steel table in the dining room. That duality suits the overall scheme perfectly.

With a house so dominated by glass, the indoor-outdoor connection is of utmost importance. Concrete blade walls run continuously from exterior to interior to exterior, thereby connecting the property from the motor court to the infinity pool, which hovers at the end of the landscape. From inside, these walls also lead the eye outward to the verdant lawn, making the outdoor palette an important factor in the interior scheme. For the primary suite, we kept the colors soft and edges rounded to create a comfortable space that complemented the cinematic views out the windows and to the garden beyond while creating a cocoon-like environment. To maximize the view from the bath and eliminate obstructions, we sank the tub. It's in decisions like these that interior designers can celebrate an architectural marvel while also allowing it to function as someone's home.

PAGE 56 AND PREVIOUS: Modernist architecture called for highly sculptural furnishings as well as a reverence for concrete and glass as the dominant materials inside and out. **ABOVE AND OPPOSITE:** In the living area, a curved sofa with bronze detail was created to soften the edges of the Brutalist-influenced architecture. Vintage Milo Baughman chairs, an Ib Kofod-Larsen lounge chair, and a polished stone cocktail table carved in Italy have a similar effect. A Wolfgang Stiller sculpture surveils the room. **OVERLEAF:** A painting by John Millei presides over the dining room. The polished base of the Magni Home Collection table multiplies the leggy chairs that surround it.

VOGUE
THE ALLURE OF BEAUTY

PREVIOUS, LEFT: Concrete and steel, in the form of Warren Platner chairs and table, make for an ideal material pairing. **PREVIOUS, RIGHT:** The glassy box of the client's office is visible as you enter the home. The custom-designed Magni Home Collection desk has a sculptural quality that lives up to the prominence of the space's location. **LEFT:** Primary colors bring an unexpected jolt of energy to the breakfast room and contrast the raw concrete walls.

KATE MOSS

OPPOSITE: In the primary suite, neutral tones create a quiet space and direct attention toward the extraordinarily lush plantings beyond the immense windows. **ABOVE:** A Japanese-style soaking tub, flanked by bronze Magni Home Collection stools, is perfectly situated to take advantage of the garden view.

RIGHT: A shaded outdoor living area protects guests from the Texas heat. The monumental poured-in-place concrete firepit is a natural gathering place in the evening. **OVERLEAF:** When designing the interiors of a modernist residence, it's critical to consider how furniture will appear both inside the space as well as from beyond the house's glass walls.

BEVERLY HILLS

ART HOUSE

My deep passion for art touches everything I do. It's evident in each project we design, but the greatest showcase for this obsession is my own house in Beverly Hills. At 2,500 square feet, it's as much a home as it is a small museum. The midcentury structure was designed by Marvin Beck in 1964, but over the years a series of owners had taken liberties with the architect's original intent. Before starting my designs, I tracked down Beck, who although retired was thrilled to share his insights on how I planned to revive his vision for a clean, open floor plan. I find that this kind of flow is also best suited for displaying art, providing long sight lines for viewing works from afar before moving in for closer inspection.

Using the rather small entry to my advantage, I hung a large-scale Kehinde Wiley portrait on a diminutive wall. It's my favorite piece in my collection and seeing it daily in such a bold manner fills me with absolute joy. Additionally, the vivid colors on such a sizable canvas in this contained space makes for a dramatic prelude of what's to come.

In the living room, I pulled back a ceiling that had been added to reveal the original post-and-beam structure, which made the perfect framework for the lighting. While many opt for recessed, I believe track systems are best for true collectors, who need the flexibility for works that are constantly being swapped out and moved around. A slab of Haisa marble running the height of the fireplace wall creates a punctuating backdrop for a Tomás Saraceno mobile. There's something so hypnotic about his work, and its open volumes and reflective surfaces keep the large sculpture from overwhelming the space. Furnishings, all in quiet colors, seemingly recede and allow the eye to focus on the collection. A Joel Morrison sculpture, Annie Lapin painting, and Erin Shirreff work on paper adorn the seating area, which is furnished with a Magni Home Collection stainless-steel coffee table and classic sofa, Cedric Hartman side tables, and Mies van der Rohe Barcelona daybed, all grounded on a brown silk rug with shimmering striations. Across the room, a Jonathan Apgar painting is paired with a Jaume Plensa bust. A moment of color is provided by a pair of teal Warren Platner chairs.

For me, the bedroom is an all-important space. I designed it as a cocoon of luxury where I can focus on reading, watching movies, sketching, even having dinner. Quite frankly, I really don't use the other rooms except for entertaining. With that in mind, I expanded the primary suite—turning the guest bedroom into a dressing room, then wrapped the entire space in a rich walnut. Floor-to-ceiling glass on one wall gives a connection to nature with a view out to the small garden I created based on the magnificent ones I visited in Kyoto, complete with small boulders, water features, and a selection of greenery appropriate to Asian culture including an extraordinary bonsai. In terms of furniture, the leather-wrapped Benedict bed from the Magni Home Collection, with attached nightstands and hidden storage compartments, serves as the anchor, as well as our museum bench, which just feels right at the foot of any bed.

Of course, in my home there is a lot of art to pack into such a small space, but it's still tightly edited. Every piece gets its moment to shine, and nothing ever feels cramped. The overall effect is pure tranquility. Such is the beauty and joy of a masterfully curated home.

—JAMES MAGNI

PREVIOUS: A vibrant canvas by Kehinde Wiley, *Archangel Gabriel*, sets the art-driven scene as soon as you enter. **RIGHT:** A Tomás Saraceno sculpture commands attention in the living room. Overhead, the post-and-beam construction is a perfect host for art lighting. Other works in the room include, from left, a sculpture by Jaume Plensa, a work on paper by Erin Shirreff, a painting by Annie Lapin, and a sculpture by Joel Morrison.

OPPOSITE: A Jonathan Apgar painting fills the wall in front of a pair of Warren Platner chairs. **ABOVE:** Sculptures by Joel Morrison and Tomás Saraceno are in dialogue with a print by April Gornik.

LEFT: A canvas by Brian Fahlstrom occupies practically an entire wall of the dining area. **ABOVE:** The garden provides a mediative escape, complete with a bonsai tree and water feature.

LEFT AND ABOVE: The primary bedroom and accompanying dressing room are sheathed in walnut wood to create a cocoon-like environment. **OVERLEAF:** When designed with the same consideration and overall approach as any indoor room, outdoor spaces rise to another level of comfort and usability.

100 INTERIORS AROUND THE WORLD
CALIFORNIA CONTEMPORARY
ESCAPES

LOS ANGELES

MAXIMUM IMPACT

Built in 1923 in the Hancock Park neighborhood of Los Angeles, this originally 1,400-square-foot home had very little curb appeal prior to its renovation. It needed a special buyer, and that's where I came in. For me, it was easy to envision how its faux-Spanish roots could be stripped away to reveal its simple-yet-clean architecture. Because there were no redeeming qualities that I was concerned about preserving, I had the freedom to transform the home into a contemporary jewel box for my wife and me.

At Magni Kalman, I don't often have the opportunity to flex my ability to maximize small spaces. We typically work on a much larger scale, but there's such satisfaction and so much to be said for making every single inch sing and every small detail a masterpiece. I added tall, linear windows along the street-facing facades to provide filtered views, to visually elongate the height of the eight-foot ceilings, and to lend architectural character. As an added benefit, the windows create a beautiful shadow play that moves throughout the course of the day.

Many designers speak of their own homes as a laboratory for ideas, and this was certainly that—a place that allows me to try out new ideas or more experimental techniques. But it wasn't as if I didn't have a client: I had my wife's tastes to consider. One of the first purchases we made was the Paul Evans cocktail table. I showed it to her thinking there was no way she was going to like it, but I was pleasantly surprised that she loved it. That piece then became the starting point for the whole living area. While I may have the stronger design aesthetic, it was still important to know how she wanted things to function. We moved in two weeks after our wedding, so the planning was also very much about how we saw our family possibly growing over time and how we wanted to entertain overnight guests in the house's two bedrooms, plus a casita.

For the interiors, an achromatic palette of warm grays, blacks, and whites allows the eye to rest—expanding the scale by making all the space more congruous. Materials selected follow the same philosophy and keep things streamlined. Other furniture decisions play into this as well, such as opting for a dining table I designed with a glass surface to keep the visual volume low. In an unexpected design twist, the base is plywood but sanded and lacquered for a refined finish. Above, the pendant chandelier is so narrow, it almost disappears.

Works by emerging and established artists such as John Millei, Aldo Chaparro, and Jonathan Apgar mingle alongside a growing collection of Brutalist and midcentury designs by Gae Aulenti and Vico Magistretti, as well as pure contemporary furnishings by Magni Home Collection. Custom pieces of my own design echo my passion for Brutalism as well as my studies in mechanical engineering. I developed the perforated aluminum sideboard with my father, who is a CNC machinist.

At every turn, there's proof that I used my home as a testing ground for new designs and for finding infinite ways to make a small space look and function as if it's larger. In the living room, I wanted to create the illusion of a fireplace and that centering feeling that a hearth brings to a room, so I added a large slab of Pietra marble to one wall. Skylights overhead draw the eye upward. In the bedroom, a large-scale sliding glass door makes that wall vanish, while I cheated the height by keeping the headboard low to make the ceiling seem higher. I also added drawers beneath the bed for additional storage.

While the scale might not be as great, there are many through lines to our work at Magni Kalman here. For example, buying what you love and balancing that with ingenuity always makes for the best results—regardless of the budget or the square footage. Additionally, although not having a lot of space requires you to really edit, there's no interior that can't benefit from that same rigor. And of course, there's always room for invention.

—JASON KALMAN

PREVIOUS: A work by Abdul Mazin hangs at the entrance to the primary suite. **RIGHT:** In the living room, tall, narrow windows maximize light while allowing privacy from the street. A dazzling Aldo Chaparro wall sculpture dominates the room while a sculptural Paul Evans cocktail table anchors a monochromatic seating area. **OVERLEAF, LEFT:** Fumed gray wood floors unify the living space. Vico Magistretti chairs are a midcentury find from a dealer in the Netherlands. **OVERLEAF, RIGHT:** The galley kitchen opens to the terrace, maximizing light and the connection to the garden.

PREVIOUS, LEFT: A small powder room packs a design punch with a cohesive mix of materials, including cerused wood, perforated aluminum, and Pietra marble. A black-and-white photograph by Hiroshi Yamazaki reinforces the tones of the room. **PREVIOUS, RIGHT:** In the dining room, a custom sideboard is made of perforated aluminum. **RIGHT:** The primary bedroom features a signature Magni Kalman all-in-one furniture piece that combines a bed and side tables. **OVERLEAF:** To extend the home's small footprint, outdoor areas are treated as fully functioning rooms and designed with the same rigor as indoor ones. The guest casita, at left, is unified with the main structure across the thoughtfully conceived outdoor room.

NEWPORT BEACH

REINVENTION

Sometimes clients ask for a refresh of a project, but it's extraordinarily rare to reimagine the same home for an entirely new client. We were fortunate enough to have this experience for a remarkable waterfront home in Newport Beach. Having designed this house from the ground up for the original owner, we were thrilled to receive a call from its new steward, who had come across our first book, *Magni Modernism*, during the real estate transaction. Not only did the new owner relate to the designs featured, but he also connected with James on a personal level, sharing a hometown of Omaha, Nebraska.

A perfect mix of indoor-outdoor living in classic California fashion, the overall design had a flexible nature that could pivot to reflect the client's program requests, which included a softer palette than the previous high-contrast, black-and-white scheme. This shift transformed the overall feel from drama to understatement. To achieve this, we replaced dark woods and monochromatic furnishings with a more optimistic tone-on-tone and lighter palette. This change helps to blur the line between indoor and outdoor with an interior courtyard and views of Balboa Bay. The doors around the courtyard can be fully pocketed to make the transition seamless. We continued this feeling by running the same travertine floor throughout and using the same Paola Lenti furniture inside and out. As a focal point of the courtyard, we installed a Jennifer Steinkamp digital artwork of flowers moving in the breeze in the style of sixteenth-century Dutch Master paintings. These alterations solidify this space as the hub of the home and an extension of the interior—rather than a glassed-off space to look out on as they too often become. This change perfectly aligns with the wish of the homeowner, who lives primarily in the Midwest, to take advantage of the California weather while here.

That California spirit continues in the interiors, which are drenched in the terrific play of colors that come from oceanfront light. The open floor plan flows freely from living room to dining room to kitchen, which was retrofitted with sleek white cabinetry and accents of stainless steel. Magni Home Collection pieces, such as the Henry sofa, Eclipse side table, Hans buffet and console, and Jewel side table, make up much of the furniture plan. The bedroom adds to the creams and silvers with hints of pale mauve. The built-in bed, backed with a wall lined with an Ultrasuede fabric, as well as photographs by Mona Kuhn, delicately reflect that hue as does our Joanna bench, which we kitted out with trays that can be used for breakfast in bed or late-night snacks.

Downstairs serves as the entertaining area in the evening, so materials get richer and reflect a nighttime vibe. The art certainly adds to the mood with a large image by Lluís Barba depicting celebrities including Jon Hamm, Scarlett Johansson, and Kim Kardashian with famous artworks among them. But no matter the time of day, this home invites visitors to move throughout the space with ease—meandering from inside to outside, taking in the boats on the water, the art collection, and the sculptural tree in the courtyard.

PAGE 98: The ultimate expression of indoor-outdoor living, this home in Corona del Mar blurs the line between the two seamlessly. **PREVIOUS:** The reinvention of this home included replacing dark wood details with white for a monochromatic, International Style look. **ABOVE:** The same Paola Lenti outdoor furniture is used inside and out for a unified visual experience. **OPPOSITE:** A digital wall installation by artist Jennifer Steinkamp illuminates the atrium and is reflected in the water below.

PREVIOUS: The courtyard plays on all the senses with a rippling water feature, a warm fire pit, expanses of travertine floor, and a sculptural tree. **ABOVE:** The open floor plan allows for multiple vantage points of the interior and courtyard, including this one from the dining table. The portrait is by Mary Borgman and the work at right is by Michael Buscemi. **OPPOSITE:** Low-slung furniture maximizes the views of Newport Beach. The wall-mounted bronze sculpture is by Anthony Pearson.

ABOVE: A sleek kitchen mixes Caeserstone and onyx with dazzling vistas. **OPPOSITE:** A seating group of Paola Lenti chairs looks out over the bay.

A symphony of pinks, mauves, and grays makes up the soothing palette of this bedroom. At the foot of the bed, a Magni Home Collection bench is furnished with trays that are as functional as they are beautiful. A photograph by Mona Kuhn graces the wall while, outside, a large-scale ceramic sculpture by Jun Kaneko presides over the terrace.

A tongue-in-cheek photograph by Lluís Barba, which includes a wide range of celebrities, sets the tone in the luxurious entertainment room.

LEFT: Ample seating options are arrayed on the terrace, which overlooks the action at the harbor below. **OVERLEAF:** An aerial view displays how terraces enhance every level of the home.

BEVERLY HILLS

PERFECT PAIRING

High up in the Trousdale section of Beverly Hills, a compound sits like a Greek temple on the mountain—a shrine to pristine design, to pure lines, and ultimately to perfection. We began the project creating a home for a client that catered to his exacting needs—as someone who adheres to precision and excellence in all aspects of life, and also who has an extensive art collection. When the house next door became available, he snapped it up with the idea that he could use the second as the ultimate entertaining complex—a place to invite friends as well as other art patrons to display his trove without having to inflict any state of disarray on his primary residence. Together, these two postwar structures, now stripped down to their purest forms, convey a presence that's both ethereal and majestic.

From the beginning, we knew that the second phase had to extend the narrative, making the pair of buildings feel intertwined even though local regulations didn't allow for them to be physically connected. In this project, executing both the architecture and design, we were able to take all of the rigor of the first and push it that much further. Instead of eliminating superfluous details and unnecessary decorative flourishes, we set out to devise something akin to a seamless glove, a creation so precise it can be turned inside out and still appear flawless. We even pushed the boundaries of an open floor plan, fashioning a six-thousand-square-foot house with only three closed rooms.

This seemingly simple white box brims with meticulous details coupled with super refined materials—all utilized as the ultimate backdrop for art, the curation of which we worked on with art consultant and longtime collaborator Michael Thomas. As you arrive in the motor court, a cutout overhead and black reflecting pool below maximize the impact of a shining Joel Morrison sculpture. In the living area, the eye moves past an array of Magni Home Collection furniture that evokes the Bauhaus to the powerful backdrop of a large-scale work by Jeff Elrod. Directly opposite, a floor-to-ceiling fireplace surround in textured white Carrara marble contrasts with the shimmering surface of an Anish Kapoor. Outside, the dramatic city view beyond becomes the perfect frame for Chris Burden's *Small Steps Skyscraper* sculpture.

None of these design decisions command attention—instead they amplify the impact of the entire experience. We call this approach the "non-detail," and it's very challenging to execute. The more you strip away, the more perfect and precise everything must be. This house combines the rigorous discipline and the kind of mathematical approach of the ancient Greeks and Romans, the Bauhaus, and International Style modernism. The resulting effect aligns with our client's deep New Age spirituality and quest to have intention behind everything. For us, a dream client is one who will go the distance. In this case, he exceeded that.

PAGE 118: The simplicity and purity of the entrance sets the stage for the minimalist drama throughout this special project. **PREVIOUS:** The side-by-side projects are connected in spirit and design. **LEFT AND ABOVE:** The powerful entry court leads the eye toward the glass doors. The placement of a shimmering Joel Morrison sculpture to the left of the entrance, in a dark reflecting pool, eschews the common practice of siting a sculpture in the center of the motor court.

Tom Kundig

PREVIOUS: In the living room, works by Tara Donovan (left) and Jeff Elrod set the stage for an array of monochromatic furniture by Magni Home collection and Knoll. **ABOVE:** With an overall scheme of sleek furniture mixed with powerful art, such as the Anish Kapoor wall sculpture (left) and Jeff Elrod painting above the fireplace, spaces flow seamlessly from one into another. **OPPOSITE:** On the far end of the entertaining space, the kitchen all but disappears with its custom white acrylic cabinetry devoid of hardware.

PREVIOUS, LEFT: A pair of Eames lounge chairs quietly complement an artwork by Giuseppe Penone. **PREVIOUS, RIGHT:** An Anish Kapoor sculpture flips the scene in the striking room. **LEFT AND ABOVE:** A glass wall and wet area encased in glass create a spa-like environment in the bath, which showcases a custom-made Caesarstone tub. The sculpture is by Joel Morrison.

OPPOSITE AND ABOVE: On the terrace, furniture is strategically placed below the zigzagging awning. A black-tiled pool creates a striking juxtaposition to the almost all-white terrace.

LEFT AND ABOVE: A towering sculpture by Chris Burden is placed in a bed of river stones. **OVERLEAF:** This perfectionist's paradise is immaculately maintained at all times to preserve its crisp design aesthetic.

NEWPORT BEACH

REINVIGORATING PAST AND PRESENT

When clients purchased a 1920s Cape Cod–style house in Newport Beach that had been in the family for generations, they came to us with a challenge. They wanted to preserve its architectural charm—and the memories it held—while making it livable for today. What many would have deemed a teardown, we viewed instead as an opportunity to connect past and present. The homeowners' modern needs called for more square footage and more flexibility for children, grandchildren, and visiting friends. Initially they imagined the project to be a light remodel of the five-bedroom house. In the end, we took things down to the studs and enlisted EBTA Architects for some of the restructuring needs.

As a firm, our style does not lean toward the classical or traditional, so this project allowed us to stretch our range while staying true to our design philosophy. In keeping with our preference for open-plan spaces, we edited out walls and extraneous decoration to establish a purer version of the original structure. We exercised restraint to preserve the home's integrity and added our own take, such as the addition of traditional white oak casework throughout, which nods to the home's past while bringing in warmth. As a result, the house exudes sophistication without even a whiff of stuffiness.

The clients are a breezy, barefoot kind of family, and we respected that with each design decision. The contemporary portion, which is attached to the bay side of the existing house, converts into an open-air pavilion through a series of nano-walls. It contains the family room and dining area and allows for complete access to water views. These large-scale windows called for furniture to be more centralized in the space—pulling it away from the walls with everything flowing outward. In keeping with our vision, the furniture is a mix of new custom pieces and collectible vintage ones, all of them highly sculptural yet comfortable. Unexpected combinations include vintage chairs by T.H. Robsjohn-Gibbings mingling with acrylic side tables as well as Milo Baughman chairs from the 1960s surrounding a Magni Collection cocktail table with a cast-glass top. The spaces are also unified by a crisp, silvery palette, which seems almost devoid of color. For us, this choice was an intentional complement to the abundance of greenery outside, which naturally becomes part of the color scheme. We've always believed it's best not to compete with God.

From the beginning, our clients were very open about the fact that they didn't know much about art but wanted to learn more. At that time, they were just collecting Laguna seaside watercolors. So, working in partnership with their art consultants, we introduced them to contemporary artists who aligned with the overall aesthetic. They very quickly excelled at collecting and were eager students, visiting galleries, fairs, and exhibitions. Within a few years their collection came to include works by Louise Bourgeois, Tony Cragg, Kehinde Wiley, and Tara Donovan, to name a few. To complement their playful personalities, we acquired artworks with a sense of whimsy such as Jeppe Hein balloons, which are permanently suspended on the ceiling at the top of the stair, and a bronze Gavin Turk trash bag that fools many guests.

Perhaps the moment that best captures the mood of this home is a Takashi Murakami sculpture laid out on a plinth in the entry hall. The glistening silver anime figure seems transported from the future where it resides surrounded by painted brick, rounded arches, and old-fashioned lanterns hearkening back a century. The selection and placement create a unique tension that bridges the past and present, in the same way that the house beautifully exists between the 1920s and today.

PAGE 138 AND PREVIOUS: After an extensive renovation, a 1920s Cape Cod–style cottage on Balboa Peninsula in Newport Beach retains its soul while taking on an airy new life. **ABOVE:** A Tara Donovan work composed of steel-headed pins presides over a seating area of four Milo Baughman chairs situated around a Magni Home Collection cocktail table. **OPPOSITE:** T.H. Robsjohn-Gibbings armchairs give a sense of history to mostly contemporary furnishings in the reimagined living area. **OVERLEAF:** Waterfront views appear so close you can touch them as the walls and doors fold away to allow the room to function almost as a covered terrace.

LOUIS VUITTON

S VUITTON

DESIGN ≠ ART
BRANCUSI

PREVIOUS, LEFT: From its pedestal, a Kehinde Wiley sculpture looks on. **PREVIOUS, RIGHT:** In the foreground, a platinum and carbon fiber sculpture by Takashi Murakami rests supine on a plinth, while a Jaume Plensa sculpture is sited outdoors. **OPPOSITE:** An installation of mirrored Jeppe Hein sculpture is paired with a canvas by Garth Weiser in the upstairs hallway. **ABOVE:** The second floor, where the primary bedroom is located, retains some of the original charm while staying contemporary with a custom-made bed. **LEFT:** The luxurious bath in the primary suite features a pair of showers as well as a soaking tub.

RIGHT: A colorful Mark Grotjahn painting hangs near the warm wood dining table, which is paired with metal chairs with a curved, organic shape. The "trash bag" below the stairs is a bronze sculpture by Gavin Turk. **OVERLEAF, LEFT AND RIGHT:** Original brick arches not only speak to the house's 1920s character, but also perfectly frame the Jaume Plensa sculpture. **PAGES 154–55:** The house represents the perfect mix of old and new, family and art.

ATHERTON

MODERN SYNTHESIS

Our design work chiefly happens inside crisp, contemporary boxes with expanses of glass and minimal detailing. But for this project in the Bay Area, we were given the unique opportunity to explore how contemporary design can live within a classically inspired setting—combining past and present. Working with architect Richard Landry, the clients devised a house with bones that reflect the great historic estates of France. Embracing that spirit, we established an interiors concept that centered on imagining the house had stood for two hundred years and had been modernized over time. The result is a study in how to honor a wide range of eras of French design and architecture while blending them seamlessly.

Although the goal was always to remain quite contemporary, a major historical style we explored was Art Deco. We share a great affinity for the aesthetic with the clients, and this seven-year project turned into a deep dive into the exuberant lines, motifs, and materials that define the look of the 1920s and '30s. That influence is felt the moment one enters the home through the glass doors embellished with stylized ironwork and steps into the foyer. The floor—glossy white embellished with a black-and-gray pattern—sets the tone for this modern deco approach—along with the juxtaposition of a gleaming Hervé Van der Straeten console with a dramatic Murano glass chandelier, which we discovered with the clients in the Paris flea market. We found a matching pair in two different stalls and then fused them to form a twenty-two-foot showstopper. A mirror-topped, stainless-steel table on the floor below creates an almost infinite reflection, exponentially enhancing the chandelier's effect.

Unlike contemporary homes with open floor plans, this house is sectioned into individual rooms, which allowed us to create sumptuous jewel box after jewel box. Normally, we are working on larger rooms where seating areas flow together into a cohesive statement, but these defined spaces allowed us to imagine distinct experiences layered in luxury. For example, the library is wrapped in eucalyptus paneling with polished nickel inlays complemented by a parquet floor of bleached and gray oaks in a pinwheel pattern. The contents of the room are as exuberant as they are refined with an inlaid Jules Leleu cabinet facing off against a Yayoi Kusama surmounting an expressive Saint Laurent marble fireplace. The seating area between is centered by Art Deco–inspired chairs and table—but with polished John Lyle side tables to keep things from dwelling too long in the past.

Other rooms throughout the home tap into this same combination of Art Deco fabulousness tempered with minimalist modernity. The equally decadent dining room is sheathed in white gold–leafed walls and ceilings and accented by macassar ebony trim and doors. Here, the furniture silhouettes feel pared back while still of the period, as do the scaled-up checkerboard marble floors. The double-height living room serves as another example of this provocative mix, showcasing 1930s Art Deco pieces, 1960s chairs, Magni Home Collection, and contemporary furniture artists—all coexisting on top of a rug with a Jazz Age feel thanks to a pattern inspired by the client's favorite vintage watch. Every element of this project is grounded in some element of our classical training—without which we wouldn't have the flexibility to insert a modern perspective. By going back and carefully studying the history of French architecture and design, we were able to invent a language all our own.

PAGE 156: Two vintage Murano chandeliers were combined to span the home's three levels in the entry stairwell. **PREVIOUS:** A reflective, prismatic sculpture by Arik Levy challenges the French-inspired architecture in all the right ways. **LEFT:** Collectible furniture by Hervé van der Straeten punctuates the foyer, which is defined by the graphic detail in its marble floor.

ABOVE AND OPPOSITE: While grilled dormer windows draw the eyes up in the majestic living room, the height of the ceiling is brought down with moves such as dividing the fireplace into three horizontal sections and adding a pair of chandeliers. Glamour prevails with furniture with Art Deco lines. The custom rug is inspired by a piece of jewelry in the homeowner's collection.

PREVIOUS, LEFT: A thread painting of a chandelier by Kyungah Ham speaks to the glamour infusing the home as well as its impressive lighting. **PREVIOUS, RIGHT:** Smaller spaces like the library provided opportunities to introduce unexpected surprises and layer in details such as eucalyptus paneling embedded with polished nickel and complex parquet floors. Major pieces include a Jules Leleu cabinet and silver Art Deco lamps. **ABOVE AND OPPOSITE:** In the kitchen, shimmering metal details and ornate woodwork reflect the Jazz Age feel of the rest of the home. Even the breakfast and family areas have an air of luxury and formality.

PREVIOUS, LEFT: The primary bedroom, with its jewelry-like pendant by Hervé van der Straeten, reflects a contemporary take on classic French design. **PREVIOUS, RIGHT:** The bathroom's checkboard marble floor and the tub's sculpted base lend Art Deco drama. **ABOVE AND RIGHT:** A double shower surrounded by bronze-framed panels of glass leads to a private outdoor pool accessible only through the primary suite.

PREVIOUS, LEFT AND RIGHT: Outdoor rooms were carved out for hosting guests on a variety of scales. **ABOVE:** The two-story wine cellar showcases the couple's passion for collecting special vintages as well as hosting. **RIGHT:** In the dining room, walls sheathed in white gold leaf create a sultry shimmer. The custom-designed cabinets are made of cast glass and smoked mirror with white bronze legs. **OVERLEAF:** Inside and out, the design marries a desire for contemporary living with inspiring architecture and furnishings that conjure another era.

BEVERLY HILLS

COMPLETE METAMORPHOSIS

The overall look of a home has many possible outcomes. Our main role as designers is to ensure that the end result aligns with our client's vision of who they are and how they want to live. For that reason, it's such a special gift when a house we once worked on comes back to us through new ownership. That's precisely what happened to us with this home we had originally worked on with the architect Richard Landry. The sets of owners couldn't have had more different points of view, and it was fascinating to work with each of them to realize their respective visions.

The first owners wanted clean, crisp, and all-out contemporary design. Next, a British businessman and avid collector aspired to make this once quite splashy space his own while embracing the California lifestyle. We were astonished and delighted as he led us through his collection of paintings, sculpture, and design pieces. Artworks in his trove include important pre- and postwar modern art by Salvador Dalí, Joan Miró, Henry Moore, Alexander Calder, Fernand Léger, and Man Ray. To reflect the museum-quality selection, we scoured galleries, auctions, and showrooms to find the strongest examples of significant midcentury designers such as Paul Evans, Vladimir Kagan, and Edward Wormley, which we mixed with contemporary designs to help tie in the existing architecture.

Now we had to create the perfect backdrop for these phenomenal pieces, and we knew that the interior architecture had to be softened along with making some layout changes, such as reorienting the family room to take advantage of views of the city, terrace, and garden. That terrace was an important focal point for the client, who, coming from London, wanted to take advantage of the indoor-outdoor Los Angeles lifestyle and blur the line between the family room and this area. To suit this request, we opted for interior furniture covered in outdoor fabrics, an overall concept that reflected his tailored aesthetic.

Architecturally, one of the most dazzling features of the home is a unique, white marble entry wall designed by Zaha Hadid, which perfectly complements the curve of the wall and stair. The monumental addition adds a breathtaking dynamism as you enter the otherwise geometric space. Elsewhere, we made changes that brought a warm earthiness that was more aligned with our clients' tweedy, intellectual vibe. We wrapped the living room's marble fireplace in a soft plaster. We added a wood ceiling and vines to the outdoor terrace. Even something as simple as putting down a flatweave rug brought in just the right amount of texture.

It's remarkable to see how a place once so crisp and edgy could so gracefully transform into an elegantly understated home. The mix of periods and eras reflected in the collection seems at home in the contemporary space. We bridged that gap by bringing in contemporary pieces that spoke to past eras in their lines and refinement while creating a home filled with utter sophistication at every turn.

PREVIOUS: A sculpture by Salvador Dalí pairs splendidly with a William Turnbull painting above a unique Paul Evans credenza. **LEFT:** The entry sets the tone for the range of collections in the home with works by Sandra Blow, Joan Miró, and Alexander Calder, and a center table by Paul Evans.

A sculptural marble wall conceived by Zaha Hadid transforms the architecture into a work of art. A painting by Jean Dubuffet hangs near the entrance to the dining room.

CHAGALL

LEFT AND ABOVE: A soft color palette is the perfect backdrop for the homeowner's impressive collection of art, antiques, and collectible furniture, including chairs by Gianfranco Frattini and Paul Evans; sculptures by Auguste Rodin, Diego Giacometti, Henry Moore, and Georges Braque; and a painting by Roberto Matta.

OPPOSITE: In a corner of the living room, a Man Ray sculpture is displayed next to a painting by William Scott. The chair is by Paul Evans. **LEFT:** A small bronze by Henry Moore surveys the scene. **ABOVE:** In the gallery-like room are displayed paintings by Hans Hofmann (at left) and Robert Motherwell (at right) in addition to sculptures by Henry Moore and Diego Giacometti.

ABOVE: The custom kitchen is centered around a one-of-a-kind Maestro by Bonnet cooking suite, with the other functions concealed behind sleek cabinetry. **OPPOSITE:** A painting by William Turnbull is a striking addition to the otherwise neutrally toned dining room. A Tang dynasty horse sculpture is displayed on a Paul Evans credenza, joined by a Salvador Dalí sculpture to the left.

Henry Moore
MAN RAY
SURREALISM IN PARIS

OPPOSITE: A painting by Bernard Buffet, sculpture by Julio González, and a vintage tiled table make for a calming but visually rich tableau. **ABOVE:** The room also features artworks by Alexander Calder, Fernand Léger, Julio González, and Bill Brandt. A small glass-topped table by Vladimir Kagan, paired with chairs by Edward Wormley, provides a casual place to dine. **OVERLEAF:** The primary bedroom combines rosy neutrals with superluxurious textures. The metal detailing, leather paneling, and floor-to-ceiling lighting of the wall behind the bed add another level of glamour.

ABOVE AND RIGHT: The dressing room features a tabletop and drawer handles in gleaming rock quartz. **OPPOSITE:** The entire suite flows harmoniously with its cohesive scheme.

OPPOSITE AND ABOVE: His and hers baths are wrapped in contrasting marbles.

RIGHT: Lighting brings high drama to the monochromatic scheme of the cinema. **OVERLEAF:** On the terrace, Magni Home Collection sofas and chairs are comfortable places to curl up next to the custom stone firepit.

PACIFIC PALISADES

NESTING PERCH

Every young family goes through a nesting phase, when they want to ensure that every design decision helps to maximize their quality time together. But not every family has to make all of those choices from halfway around the world. For these clients, who were relocating from Hong Kong to California, that was exactly the case. Luckily, we were able to streamline their decision-making and find a clear path to blending the husband's preference for strict minimalism with the wife's passion for detail, all while allowing a touch of whimsy for the children.

Perched on a complicated hillside lot with steep topography, the house came together as a series of levels engineered to best take advantage of the sweeping canyon views while maintaining privacy from the street. Taking this into account, architectural firm ShubinDonaldson devised a unique plan with steps down to the entrance, creating a private garden before the front door. Once inside the towering pivot door, a sculptural wood staircase with a carved handrail leads up to a private floor of bedrooms, while a separate louvered staircase lands in the great room below. From a design perspective, we had the refreshing challenge of both connecting and contrasting the various levels.

Given the architectural format, each room on the canyon side faces outward, with walls of glass mixed with honey-colored wood paneling and travertine floors. In the family room, multiple functions come together. An expansive sectional sofa is situated to take in the view while not feeling too precious, and a similar floor plan is mirrored in the outdoor living area just beyond. Working in a palette that is more expressive than what we normally gravitate toward, we pulled from the blues of the sky. The dining area divides the larger room, and a wood dropped soffit overhead defines the space without using walls. The live edge table and leggy Vladimir Kagan chairs reflect the clients' preference for vintage furnishings, while the Avram Rusu lighting speaks to the wife's eye for detail, honed by a career in jewelry auctions. The kitchen, outfitted in the same combination of warm materials, seamlessly blends into the scheme without calling too much attention to itself.

A slightly more refined sensibility comes into play in the primary suite. Utilizing our signature bed machine, in which we combine the bed, nightstands, lighting, and headboard into one unit, we created a cloudlike palette with more muted wood details. The bath is a study in crisp, clean lines—echoing the rest of the home's mix of warm wood with beautiful stone. Expanses of mirror on both walls intensify the beauty of the canyon—creating the sensation that the room is entirely outdoors. That kind of immersion in the California lifestyle is exactly what this family wanted to achieve—and we were able to deliver just that from thousands of miles away.

PAGE 202: The entrance to the house sits below street level to create a hidden entry garden as well as to add a layer of privacy. **PREVIOUS, LEFT:** A sculpture by Betty Gold is framed by the view. **PREVIOUS, RIGHT:** Special carved details in both the stair treads and handrail bring a sculptural dimension to the entry. **RIGHT:** In the small living room off the entrance, Gio Ponti chairs are paired with a cocktail table from the Magni Home Collection. The view beyond shows the terraced garden that leads down to the front door.

ASIA IMAGINED
VALENTINO

CARTIER

OPPOSITE AND ABOVE: In the homeowner's office, we added a floating bookshelf and paired it with a Franco Albini desk. Along with the patterned rug, they bring warmth, patina, and texture to the room.

ABOVE AND RIGHT: Warm woods envelop the family room, which encompasses a sitting area, dining area, and kitchen.

LAROUSSE

LEFT: Walnut cabinetry brings a coziness to the kitchen, which is also accented with beveled-edge countertops. **ABOVE:** A wood ceiling above the dining table helps to define the dining space. A gemlike lighting pendant by Avram Rusu hangs above a live edge dining table, which was crafted by hand in Napa by Studio Roeper.

ABOVE: A soaking tub takes advantage of the impressive views. Wood accents link the architecture and cabinetry within a marble envelope. **RIGHT:** The primary bedroom showcases a signature all-in-one bed unit, or "bed machine," which integrates the headboard into the wall and features built-in nightstands and lamps. The effect is both soothing and organized. **OVERLEAF:** From the street, the home sinks into the site—but from the rear, the multilevel house takes advantage of views from multiple floors.

SCOTTSDALE

WARM GLOW

When people try to poke holes in modern houses, they often claim that they're too cold. This Paradise Valley, Arizona, home, located in a secluded community set beneath Camelback Mountain, proves that a modern home can be inviting, filled with personality, and even fun. Our clients came to us looking for a more edited and contemporary lifestyle after deciding to move from a sprawling Mediterranean-style family home in the area to a contemporary nine-thousand-square-foot abode. They were a bit apprehensive about leaving their traditional design aesthetic for something contemporary, but we eased them into the transition by pinpointing textures, colors, and curved shapes that exude warmth and comfort while still complementing the architecture and landscape.

That connection to the spectacular setting touches every design choice made both inside and out. Exterior materials were chosen for their ability to weather and patina in the desert climate while blending into the desert valley environment. Outside, every surface—both rough stone and oxidized metal—conveys a raw beauty that's still completely luxurious. Sculptural cacti and water features complete the effect. Once inside, the material palette continues but in a more refined manner. A sandblasted black granite wall with integrated handrail invites visitors to actually touch that connection to nature, generating a full multisensory experience as an Olafur Eliasson light sculpture casts prismatic patterns.

In the living area, ceiling slats in honey-colored wood, a shade specifically chosen to match the mountain, lead the eye directly out to the staggering view. Walnut panels flank some of the walls, their striations running horizontally and accented by bronze inlay. The furnishings complete the mood: a button-tufted velvet sofa nods to something more traditional, while a pair of curved-back Magni Home Collection chairs in an ombré alpaca fabric pick up the lavender hues of the vista. The textured silk rug continues that play on colors and textures drawn from nature.

The concept of blending into the landscape continues in the generous primary suite. Here, the seating area is enveloped in wood, again accented with panels of aged bronze. Warm gray lounge chairs sit atop a shimmering cashmere rug. A muted stripe on cashmere throw pillows is a subtle nod to the horizon. A ruched leather chair evokes a sculpture in its placement near a window and next to a blown glass floor lamp. The bedroom area is even more alluring. Pulled away from the wall, the bed floats in the space, allowing for a better view—while multiplying it with mirror panels behind the channeled headboard. Curved walnut edges, bronze details, and leather-paneled bedside tables complete this very deluxe take on a bed, which is a signature of our work.

But perhaps the best seat in the house just might be past the knife-edge pool, at the end of the terrace, around the fire pit, where four Paola Lenti chairs are arranged in a row. The lounges are sculptural without being too serious, streamlined with a comfortable approach, and have front row views of majestic scenery—just like the entire home.

LEFT: The materials of this house in Paradise Valley, Arizona—stone and oxidized metal—are the perfect reflection of its breathtaking desert landscape and bring warmth to the contemporary design. **ABOVE:** Water features appeal to the senses while adding another opportunity to reflect the stunning natural scenery.

OPPOSITE TOP: In the living room, honey-colored walnut paneling complements the colors present in the views of Camelback Mountain. **OPPOSITE BOTTOM:** The fabrics and rugs were chosen for both their palette and tactility. **ABOVE:** Low-slung furniture with sinuous lines and graceful forms, including a pair of lavender alpaca wool–covered chairs from the Magni Home Collection, has a strong presence while also maximizing the views.

LEFT: Sleek concealed cabinetry with minimalist fixtures and hardware helps the kitchen to seamlessly coexist with the living area. A collection of LED-illuminated glass pendants is suspended above a BDDW dining table, echoing the glow of the lustrous metal wall panels. **OVERLEAF, LEFT:** A refined glass vase contrasts with the craggy mountain in the distance. **OVERLEAF, RIGHT:** An illuminated handrail is carved in the sandblasted black granite wall of the stairway.

PREVIOUS: The sitting room of the spacious primary suite is outfitted in invitingly tactile materials, including alpaca and leather in a palette that reflects the soothing colors of the landscape. **OPPOSITE:** A louver system allows for privacy between the sitting area and bedroom. **ABOVE:** Bronzed mirror sits behind the bed, which is a custom design that integrates the headboard and nightstand, all sheathed in a combination of walnut and leather.

PREVIOUS: Whimsical pieces and soft shapes reflect the client's desire to execute a warmer version of contemporary design. **OPPOSITE:** The Grigio bubble onyx, rich with mauve and pink, nods to the hues of the landscape, while patinated bronze paneling casts a flattering glow. **ABOVE:** A combination of glass and mirrors in the bathroom multiplies the staggering vista.

ABOVE: A combination of bronze, pitted steel, and wood makes for a sophisticated mix of materials that can stand up to the harsh elements. **OPPOSITE:** Multiple seating areas and a multilevel swimming pool maximize options for relaxing and appreciating the mountain range. **OVERLEAF:** Sculptural chairs are lined up to take in Camelback Mountain, as well as to enjoy the fire pit.

OBJECTS

FUNCTIONAL ART

Art has existed as long as man. Not until recently, though, perhaps with Andy Warhol, has art embraced the commercial. Warhol's art was created by him but fabricated by his studio employees. To me, this sounds a bit like the making of furniture.

When I design furniture, I approach it as an artist. I see objects such as those on the following pages as finely crafted, bespoke sculptures. It's what I was trained to do, having started my studies in sculpture before transitioning to architecture and ultimately to interiors. Each piece has been created with the intent to impact our projects with the same feeling as one gets while viewing an artist's masterwork. It was my business partner, Brooke Magni, who spearheaded growing these individual artistic endeavors into a holistic assemblage of work, which we now refer to as Magni Home Collection.

I feel the best architecture and design should have a timeless quality. Classic compositions that endure are what I seek in my creative journeys. Methods and materials that stand the test of time are of great interest to me. Bronze, glass, gold, exotic woods, parchment, etc., have been used artistically for thousands of years. Today, they are so very expensive that to use them in "furniture" is costly and rare. While most furniture collections offer faux finishes such as painted bronze, synthetic wood veneers, and artificial parchment and shagreen, authenticity is non-negotiable for each object I design and present to the world. Mies van der Rohe's famous assertion that "God is in the details" is an adage around which I have framed my career and personal life.

The pieces Brooke and I create are authentic and difficult to construct; yet the end results inevitably appear simple. How does one live as a minimalist in a chaotic world? You must edit the complex into simple clarity and forms with nothing extraneous. My personal and artistic belief is that the end result speaks for itself; when something is pared down to its essence, its purest nature comes into being.

Creation requires evolving oneself to a higher place. For me, creativity requires spirituality. I'm not referring to religion, but rather anything that uplifts you to become your higher self. The universe, nature, music—creativity flows and enlightenment is obtained when I'm connected to my source. It is in this space that many artists find connection with their work.

Painting, sculpture, and photography are labeled fine art, while furniture, textiles, and wall coverings are considered decorative art. However, a painting hung on a wall in a room is just as "decorative" as a chair, despite any deeper meaning behind its creation. What we call Magni Home Collection is a series of artistic endeavors with functional purpose to be used as lighting, chairs, and tables. It is plain to see that there is not one single style across this collection, but rather pieces that were inspired by nature, architecture, fashion, music, and of course paintings and sculpture. In the end, it's all art to me.

—JAMES MAGNI

PREVIOUS: Amsterdam chair, 2010; cast bronze, silk velvet **ABOVE:** Amsterdam dining table and chairs, 2010; cast bronze, diamante glass, silk velvet

ABOVE: Amsterdam console, 2010; cast bronze, marble

LEFT: Illuminated Objects, Orbital Series, 2020; hand-blown Murano glass **ABOVE:** Three Planets Aligned, Orbital Series, 2020; hand-blown Murano glass

ABOVE: Three Planets Aligned, Orbital Series, 2020; hand-blown Murano glass
OPPOSITE: Carmel sconce, 2017; hand-cast glass, polished stainless steel

OPPOSITE: Hollywood lamp, 2020; hand-cast glass, white bronze **ABOVE:** Jewel sconce, 2011; hand-cast glass, bronze

ABOVE AND OPPOSITE: Pandora buffet, 2013; natural parchment, cast bronze, shagreen

ABOVE AND RIGHT: Colette table, 2008; cast bronze, diamante glass

ABOVE: Pyramid table, 2014; cast glass

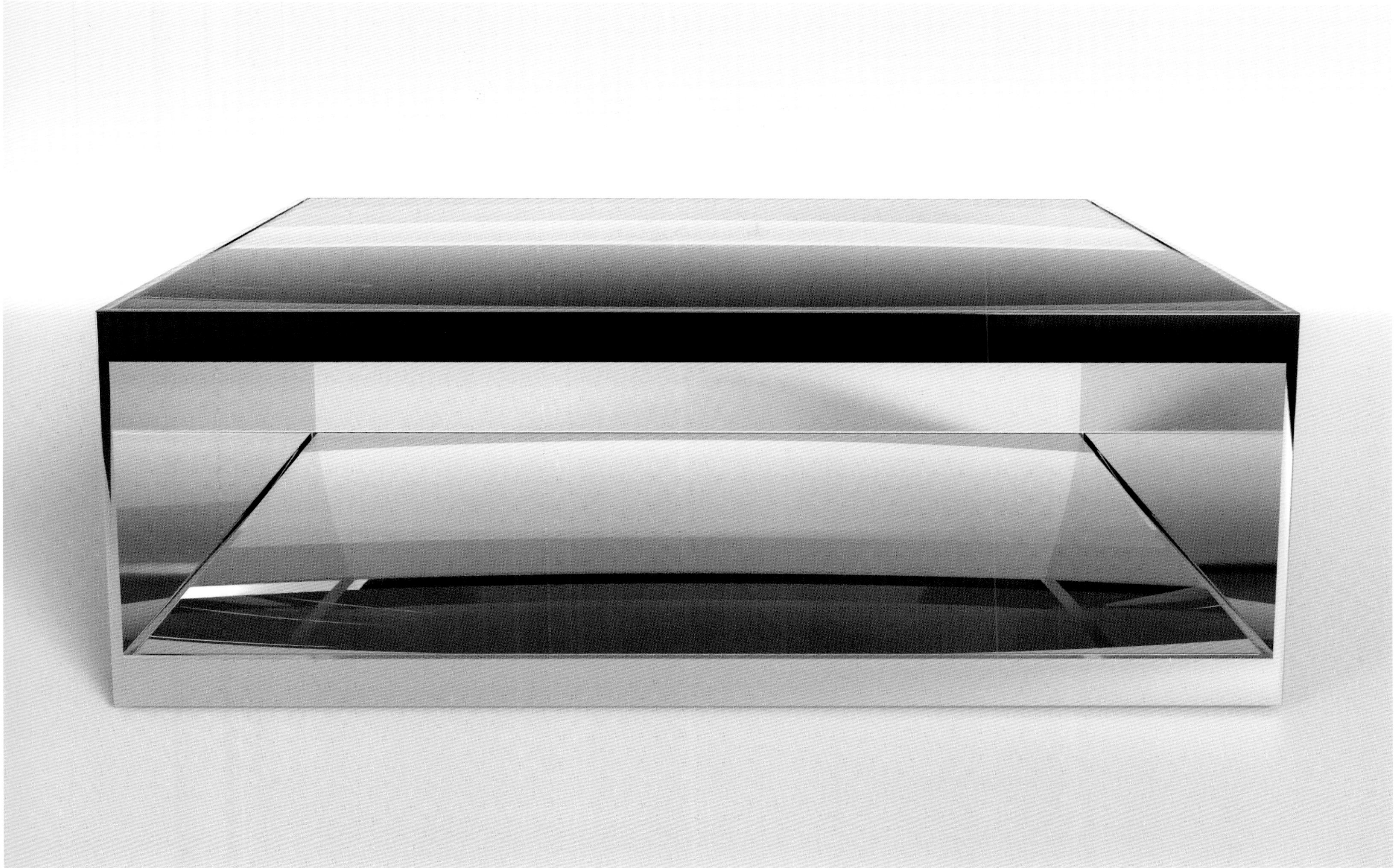

OPPOSITE: Jewel coffee table, 2005; cast glass, white gold leaf, stainless steel
ABOVE AND LEFT: Glass House table, 2005; hand-polished stainless steel, diamante glass

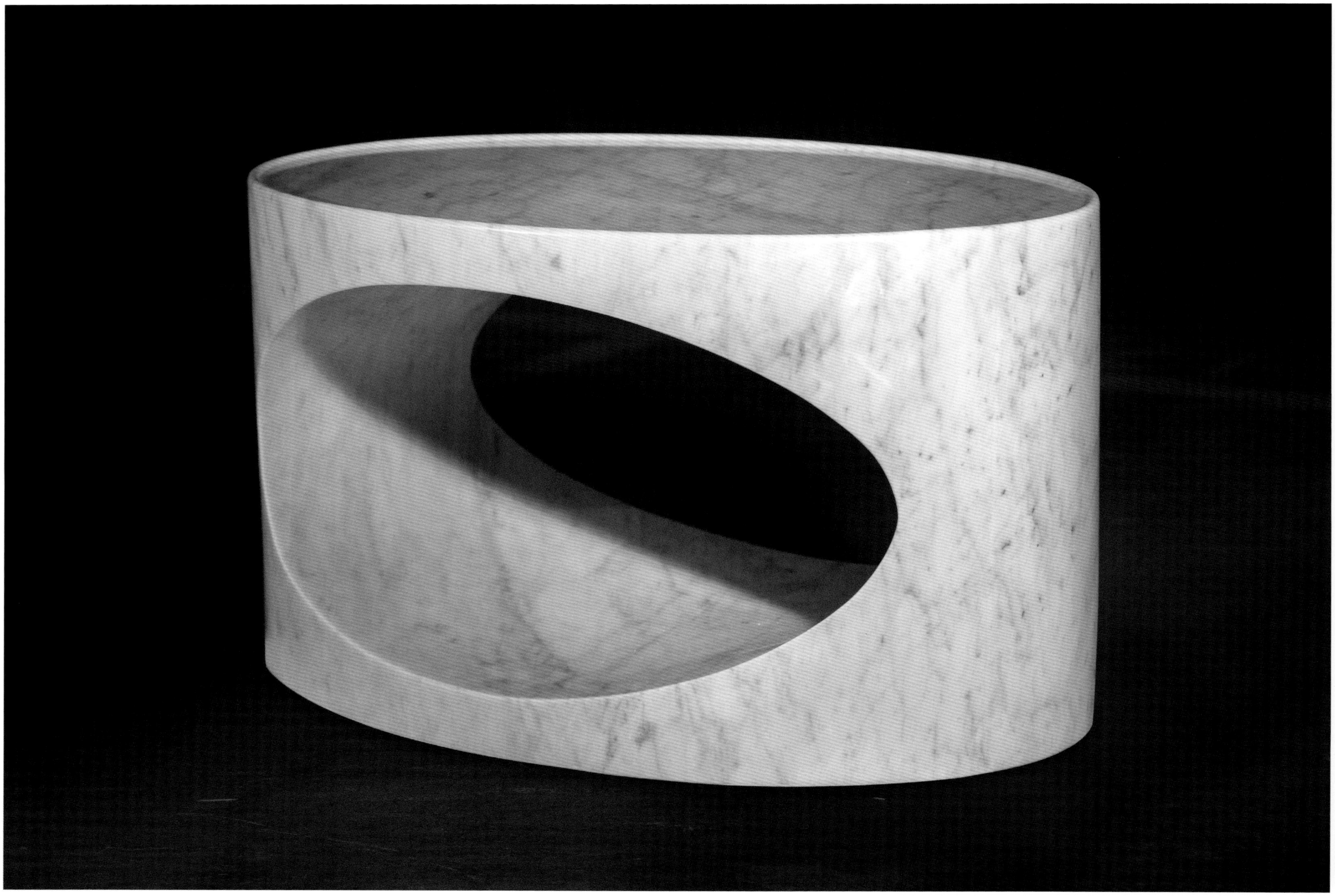

ABOVE: Olympia table, 2017; Carrara marble **RIGHT:** Athens bench, 2006; Calacatta Oro marble **OPPOSITE:** Athens, Greek, and Mykonos stools, 2005; Carrara marble

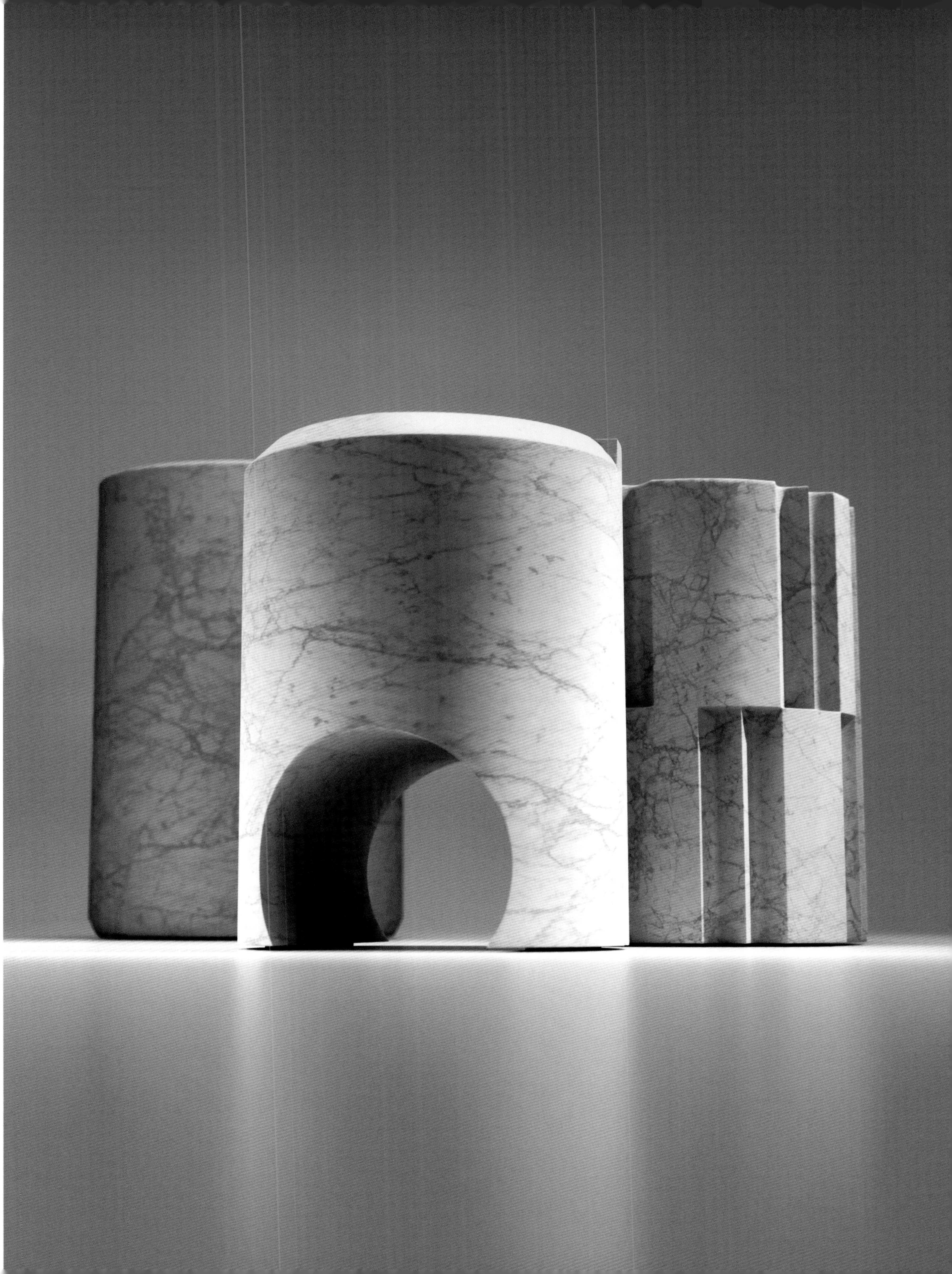

OPPOSITE: Slante and Geo vases, 2024; polished stainless steel **ABOVE:** Curva vases, 2024; silver plate **LEFT:** Manhattan vase, 2024; silver plate, rosewood

ABOVE AND OPPOSITE: Brooch mirror, 2018; cast aluminum, 14-karat gold

Skyline rug, 2010; silk

Afrikan stool, 2015; cast bronze, mahogany, leather

OPPOSITE: Harlow dining table, 2012; polished stainless steel, diamante glass
ABOVE: Mondrian chandelier, 2017; bronze, hand-blown glass

ABOVE AND OPPOSITE: Mesa dining table, 2018; hand-cast bronze, diamante glass **OVERLEAF:** Manhattan coffee table, 2012; hand-cast glass, stainless steel

DONALD SULTAN

EPILOGUE

CONTINUUM

The homes featured in this book, while unique in architectural style, scale, location, and client program, all share a commonality. Regardless of whether each interior was designed within a grand, traditional residence or a sleek, minimalist structure, there was always an importance placed on curating something greater than simply decoration. James and I share a love for past eras of design and have been blessed to travel to far-flung locations around the globe. With that comes a desire to bring a worldly and diverse influence to our interiors—but always with the focused, studied eye of a tailor.

We often speak of distilling elements within an interior to their essence, or sometimes the "anti-detail." This can apply to something as simple as a baseboard detail, or the way two materials meet in a table's design, or in the selection of furniture for a living room. There's a story from many years ago when our firm designed a space for a showcase house that exemplifies this tendency perfectly. As we stood in the corner of the room, observing guests as they took in the space, we overheard someone say, "Well, this was easy. They only picked ten pieces for the room!" And our response to this mindset is always, "Yes, but which ten pieces?!" This distillation is not a totally novel idea. There are numerous quotes from famous designers in history with which the readers of this book will be familiar: "Less is more." "Simplicity is the ultimate sophistication." "God is in the details." But these concepts remain as true today as they were then, although the way in which they are executed may be more varied and nuanced in this age of design.

The focus for all our past, current, and future work can be traced to one project that James designed thirty years ago, the Buehler Residence. The Buehler Residence provided a unique take on contemporary interior design and helped to define our style of Global Modernism. By not limiting the interior architecture and furniture to the mainstays usually associated with modern homes, it expanded the definition of what can be considered modern and added James's unique entry to the continuum of modernism. This home also showed that the combination of the finest sixteenth-century French, Art Deco, Modernist, and contemporary elements and furniture, when developed in a carefully considered manner, can create a design that is truly timeless. This timelessness is something we strive for constantly, tending to steer clear of trends, to provide our clients with sanctuaries that will age gracefully and always remain relevant. The Buehler Residence, despite being designed three decades ago, remains a project in our portfolio that regularly draws clients to our firm. It's a home that helped to shape my own personal design mantras and inclinations. And it's a design that will forever remain a touchstone as our firm pushes ahead creating new and exciting work.

Our particular brand of modernism, adding high luxury and a collected sensibility to a design style too often considered sparse and cold, is something that continues to be honed by James, me, and our like-minded and exceptionally talented team. Each new project is an opportunity to refine the essence of our design philosophy across various architectural forms. Our continued aim is for our interiors to blend seamlessly with our clients' architectural programs while luxuriously elevating their living experiences. It's through this rigorous response to architecture and curation of interiors and art that we will make our mark and push modernism forward along its continuum.

—JASON KALMAN

The Buehler Residence showcased a diverse and expansive collection of important furnishings and modern art to create a signature look that has been called Global Modernism. The home featured work by artists such as David Hockney, Sean Scully, Pat Steir, and Rebecca Purdum, situated among highly collectible antiques and modern furniture from many eras in history.

HOUSE

ABOUT US

MAGNI KALMAN

JAMES MAGNI is an American designer holding dual citizenship in Italy and the United States. After earning a degree in architecture, he established his eponymous firm, Magni Design, in 1988. He has since been recognized as one of the foremost modernist designers of our time and featured in *Architectural Digest*'s AD100, *LUXE*'s Gold List, and Robb Report's Top 40 Designers. In 1996, he created the Magni Home Collection, which showcases lighting, rugs, and furniture of his design.

JASON KALMAN is a native Californian and interior designer. He became a named partner in Magni Kalman Design in 2016, after finding his start with the firm in 2010. In addition to designing and managing residential projects that have appeared in many major publications, he oversees the day-to-day operations of the design studio in Los Angeles. He also collaborates with the Magni Home Collection team to create signature offerings within the furniture collection.

Magni Kalman has developed a style characterized by environments that simultaneously telegraph a sense of sumptuous luxury while also clearly subscribing to modernism's promise that clean lines and uncluttered spaces are instrumental in delivering serenity and comfort amid the chaos of contemporary life. Their inimitable style—rigorous, impeccable, sophisticated—has left an indelible mark on the worlds of architecture and interior design. More importantly, however, it continues to move modernism along the stylistic continuum, elevating and ushering it into a new era.

ACKNOWLEDGMENTS

A great many individuals have contributed to the creation of this book. Without them, this book would pale in comparison to what we feel has been achieved.

First and foremost, our deepest gratitude goes to our incredible clients for trusting in our process and inviting us into your lives to design these private sanctuaries. We are honored to have played a role in shaping a part of your everyday existence—it's a responsibility we have never taken lightly.

Our heartfelt appreciation to Monacelli, and especially to our amazing editor, Jenny Florence, for making this book possible. Your unwavering patience and commitment to our joint vision was inspiring. Thank you to Sam Shahid and John MacConnell for bringing the design of the book together so beautifully. And to our gurus of book publishing, Jill Cohen and Lizzy Hyland—we are eternally grateful for your steady hand and guidance from the earliest stages of this process.

To our incredibly talented Magni Kalman Design and Magni Home Collection teams: together, we are able to create design magic. While the work is not always easy, your steadfast dedication to design excellence has helped to make it all look effortless. Thank you for bringing the team's ideas to life in such inspiring ways.

We are exceptionally fortunate to collaborate with some of the greatest talents in the fields of architecture and design. To Tom Kundig, Paul McClean, Richard Landry, Russell Shubin, Scott Specht, Otoniel Solis, Bing Hu, EBTA Architects: we are beyond grateful for your inspiration in designing tremendous homes, and for your continuous support of our work.

The images on these pages showcase not only our work but also the work of photographers who are unmatched in their art. Manolo Langis, Roger Davies, and Matthew Millman, thank you for capturing the essence of our work so brilliantly. You are essential players of our extended design team. And to Mona Kuhn, as longtime admirers and collectors of your art, it is an unbelievable honor to have your work grace the cover of this book.

Our immense gratitude to the incomparable Jacqueline Terrebonne, who so gracefully lent her pen to our voices. Your ability to shape and refine our rambling thoughts on design into beautifully rational prose is astounding.

ON A PERSONAL NOTE:

To Jason's wife, Maureen; his parents, Freia and Alan; and his siblings, Eric and Danielle: thank you for your endless love, unwavering support, and sage advice. You have helped to make sense of even the most challenging times. And to Gino Graziano, you have been a true blessing to have as a guiding light in this business and in life.

To James's niece, business partner, and best friend, Brooke Magni: there are no words that can express my gratitude. Thank you. To my crazy Italian sisters, Karla and Connie, thank you for the laughs and the love. The life of an artist is not an easy one, and I appreciate my dear friends for standing by my side the whole way through.

PROJECT CREDITS

THE ART OF CRAFT

Architecture: ShubinDonaldson

Builder: Winters-Schram Associates

Landscape Design: AHBE Landscape Architects

Photography: Roger Davies

NATURAL BEAUTY

Architecture: McClean Design

Builder: Daniel Cardenas Construction

Landscape Design: M.D. Wilkes Design

Photography: Manolo Langis

CLEAR VISION

Architecture: Specht Novak Architects

Builder: Sebastian Construction Group

Landscape Design: Hocker Design

Photography: Manolo Langis

ART HOUSE

Architecture: Marvin Beck

Photography: Manolo Langis

MAXIMUM IMPACT

Architecture: Jason Kalman

Builder: D Ross Construction

Photography: Manolo Langis

REINVENTION

Architecture: Fleetwood Joiner

Builder: PMR Construction

Landscape Design: MDZA

Photography: Manolo Langis

PERFECT PAIRING

Architecture: Otoniel Solis Inc. (with Magni Kalman Design)

Builder: Cumming Group

Photography: Matthew Millman

REINVIGORATING PAST AND PRESENT

Architecture: EBTA Architects

Builder: Falcone Construction

Landscape Design: G. Grisamore Design

Photography: Manolo Langis

MODERN SYNTHESIS

Architecture: Landry Design Group

Builder: Dugally Oberfeld

Landscape Design: Robert E. Truskowski, Inc.

Photography: Matthew Millman

COMPLETE METAMORPHOSIS

Architecture: Landry Design Group

Builder: McCoy Construction

Landscape Design: Robert E. Truskowski, Inc.

Photography: Roger Davies

NESTING PERCH

Architecture: ShubinDonaldson

Builder: Tyler Development

Landscape Design: Bosky Landscape Architecture

Photography: Manolo Langis

WARM GLOW

Architecture: Bing Hu

Builder: Nance Construction

Landscape Design: Berghoff Design Group

Photography: Manolo Langis

ART CREDITS

Cover, 110–11 © Mona Kuhn; 11 Sean Scully, Landline Blue, 2013 © Sean Scully; 12, 14 © Iva Gueorguieva; 18 Rebecca Horn, Wirbelsäulen Orakel (Vertebrae Oracle), 2014, Rebecca Horn © 2025 Artists Rights Society (ARS), New York / VG Bild-Kunst, Bonn; 19 left Albert Oehlen © 2025 Artists Rights Society (ARS), New York / DACS, London; 19 right Koo Hyunmo, Paper Mulberry, 2013; 24 © Ryan Sluggett; 25 Pia Fries © 2025 Artists Rights Society (ARS), New York / VG Bild-Kunst, Bonn; 27 Najia Mehadji © 2025 Artists Rights Society (ARS), New York / ADAGP, Paris; 36, 37 Jeppe Hein, Geometric Mirrors X, 2019; 38, 42, 76–77 center © Tomás Saraceno; 44–45 © Jocelyn Marsh; 46 left, 47 left Callum Innes, Paris Blue; 46 right, 76–77 right © Annie Lapin; 47 right © Jean-Baptiste Bernadet; 49 © LeeAnn Brook; 52–53 © Jose Davila; 58–59, 61, 62 left Wolfgang Stiller © 2025 Artists Rights Society (ARS), New York / VG Bild-Kunst, Bonn; 60 left Donald Martiny © 2025 Donald Martiny / Artists Rights Society (ARS), New York; 62–63 right © John Millei; 65 left © Timothy Harding; 65 right Donald Sultan © 2025 Donald Sultan / Artists Rights Society (ARS), New York; 66–67 © Jason Willaford; 74 left, 138 left, 142 left, 144–45 right, 146 left © Kehinde Wiley; 74 center, 76–77 left © Erin Shirreff; 76–77 far left, 78 right, 147 background, 153, 154-55 Jaume Plensa © 2025 Artists Rights Society (ARS), New York / VEGAP, Madrid; 76–77 far right, 79 left, 122–23, 123 left, 140–41 center right, 143, 144–45 left © Joel Morrison; 78 left © Tomory Dodge; 79 center © April Gornik; 79 center © Jonathan Apgar; 80, 81 © Brian Fahlstrom; 86 top © Abdul Mazid; 88–89 left © Aldo Chaparro; 88–89 right © Trish DeMasi; 92 © Hiroshi Yamazaki; 93 © Dorota Jedrusik; 94 © Laura Knell; 100–101, 102 far right, 106 left © Mary Borgman; 100–101 left, 102 right, 106 far left, 107, Anthony Pearson, Untitled, bronze relief with cobalt patina, © Anthony Pearson. Courtesy of the artist and Marianne Boesky Gallery, New York and Aspen; 102 left, Callum Innes, Paris Blue; 103 © Jennifer Steinkamp; 106 right © Michael Buscemi; 110–11 left, 114–15 © Jun Kaneko; 112–13, 116–17 © Lluís Barba; 123 right © Charline von Heyl; 124–25 left, 136–37 center right, 138 left, 140–41 left, 142 right, 146 right © Tara Donovan; 124–25 center below © Jacob Kassay; 124–25 center above, 126 right, 136–37 right © Jeff Elrod; 126 left, 129, 135 right, 136–37 left Anish Kapoor © Anish Kapoor. All Rights Reserved, DACS, London/ ARS, NY 2025; 128, 130–31, 136–37 right Giuseppe Penone © 2025 Artists Rights Society (ARS), New York / ADAGP, Paris; 134–35, 135, back cover Chris Burden © 2025 Chris Burden / licensed by The Chris Burden Estate and Artists Rights Society (ARS), New York; 140–41 right, 150–51 left © Mark Grotjahn; 147 foreground, 152 Takashi Murakami, Naked Self-Portrait with Pom, © 2025 Takashi Murakami / Kaikai Kiki Co., Ltd. All Rights Reserved; 148 left, Jeppe Hein, Mirror Balloons V (dark blue, turquoise, pink, hyacinth, light blue), 2015; 148 right Garth Weiser; 150–51 center Tony Cragg © 2025 Artists Rights Society (ARS), New York / VG Bild-Kunst, Bonn; 150–51 center right, 150–51 right © Joyce Pensato; 150–51 left © Gavin Turk; 158–59 © Arik Levy; 160–61 left © Jeff Koons; 160–61 right, 164 © Kyungah Ham; 165 © Richard MacDonald; 167 © Miya Ando; 174–75 © Carlos Cruz-Diez; 176–77 left © Chuck Close; 176–77 right Yayoi Kusama, Megu-chan, Heisei period, 2014, fiberglass-reinforced plastic and paint, © Yayoi Kusama; 178 left, 189 left Salvador Dalí © 2025 Salvador Dalí, Fundació Gala-Salvador Dalí, Artists Rights Society; 178 right, 189 right William Turnbull © 2025 Artists Rights Society (ARS), New York / DACS, London; 180–81 top, 191 left Alexander Calder © 2025 Calder Foundation, New York / Artists Rights Society (ARS), New York; 180–81 center Joan Miro © Successió Miró / Artists Rights Society (ARS), New York / ADAGP, Paris 2025; 180–81 right Sandra Blow © The Sandra Blow Estate Partnership. All Rights Reserved, DACS, London / ARS, New York; 182–83 left © Jean Dubuffet; 182–83 right, 188 Damien Hirst © Damien Hirst and Science Ltd. All rights reserved / DACS, London / ARS, NY 2025; 184–85 center, 187 center Diego Giacometti © Succession Alberto Giacometti / Artists Rights Society (ARS), NY 2025; 184–85 center left © Roberto Matta; 184–85 center right, 187 bottom Henry Moore © The Henry Moore Foundation. All Rights Reserved, DACS 2025 / www.henry-moore.org; 184–85 right Georges Braque; 186 left Man Ray © Man Ray 2015 Trust / Artists Rights Society (ARS), NY / ADAGP, Paris 2025; 186 right © William Scott; 187 center left Hans Hofmann, With permission of the Renate, Hans & Maria Hofmann Trust / Artists Rights Society (ARS), New York; 187 right Robert Motherwell © 2025 Dedalus Foundation, Inc. / Artists Rights Society (ARS), NY; 190 top Bernard Buffet © 2025 Artists Rights Society (ARS), New York / ADAGP, Paris; 190 bottom, 191 center left Fernand Leger © 2025 Artists Rights Society (ARS), New York / ADAGP, Paris; 191 center right Julio González © 2025 Artists Rights Society (ARS), New York; 191 right © Bill Brandt; 204 © Betty Gold; 206–7 © Christina Craemer; 224–25 Olafur Eliasson, Slow Light, 2018, Courtesy of the artist and Tanya Bonakdar Gallery, New York/Los Angeles; 227 Olafur Eliasson, Colour experiment no. 65, 2019, Courtesy of the artist and Tanya Bonakdar Gallery, New York/Los Angeles; 230, 232–33 © Dashiell Manley.

PHOTOGRAPHY CREDITS

Mona Kuhn, cover, back cover; Manolo Langis, 4, 32–117, 138–55, 202–39, 258–259; Roger Davies, 6–31, 178–201; Matthew Millman, 118–37, 156–77; Natalia Knezevic, 240, 243–251, 253–254, 256, 260–61, 264–65, 267–69; Coup D'etat, 242; Kessia Embry, 249; David Daigle, 252, 270–71; Mike Allen, 266, 276–77; Mary Nichols, 272–75

Copyright © 2025 James Magni, Jason Kalman and the Monacelli Press

All rights reserved. No part of this book may be reproduced, stored in a retrieval system, or transmitted in any form, by any means, including mechanical, electric, photocopying, recording, or otherwise, without the prior written permission of the publisher.

Library of Congress Control Number: 2024952279

ISBN 9781580936804

Designed by Sam Shahid
Art Directed by John MacConnell, Shahid / Kraus & Company

Printed in China

Monacelli
A Phaidon Company
111 Broadway
New York, New York 10006
monacellipress.com